Juicing Recipe Book

Easy Juice Remedies for Quick Weight Loss, Detox, Energy, and Focus

Free Bonus: I really appreciate your purchase of my book and I'd like to give you another guide that I wrote which is a perfect companion to this book: *Easy Small Sprouts (http://bit.ly/sprouting-guide)*.

It will show you with full color images, the simple methods I use to grow the healthiest food I know: sprouts. Living sprouts are the pinnacle of raw foods in my opinion, so I hope you'll start adding these low cost, easy to grow, nutritional powerhouse foods to your juices and meals today.

Copyright © 2013 by Jon Symons
All rights reserved. This book or any portion thereof may not be reproduced or used in any manner whatsoever without the express written permission of the publisher except for the use of brief quotations in a book review.

Printed in the United States of America.

First Printing, 2013

If you have any questions or comments, contact me at **jon@jonsymons.com** or at my blog **JonSymons.com**, I'm very happy to hear from you and help out any way I can. You can see all of my books on my Amazon Author page: http://bit.ly/jon-symons-amazon

I'm very grateful to my sister Christina for providing the amazing cover photography: http://ChristinaSymons.com/

Disclaimer

The information in this book reflects the author's opinions and is not intended to replace medical advice. The information and recipes are for informational and educational purposes only.

Before beginning this or any nutritional program, consult your doctor to be sure it is appropriate for you. If you are unsure of any foods or methods mentioned, you should always defer to your physician's advice.

The author has made every effort to supply accurate information in the creation of this book. The author makes no warranty and accepts no responsibility for any loss or damages arising from the use of the contents of this book.

The reader assumes all responsibility for the use of the information in this text.

Table of Contents

Introduction 2
Why Juicing? 3
   Juicing is Better than Vitamin Pills 3
   Green Juice 4
   Protein in Juice? 5
Juicing for Weight Loss 6
Juice Fasting 9
Juicing Precautions 12
   Fruit Sugar – A Concern 12
   Food Combining & How to Drink Juice ... 13
   Juicing for Kids 16
Juicing Equipment 18
   Recommended Juicer Models 20
How to Buy Your Produce 24
   11 Foods you Must Buy Organic 24
   11 Foods that are Okay, Even if they're Not Organic 26
The Real Superfood: "Live" Green Juice 30
   My Easy Sprouting System 31
Prepare your Produce for Juicing 36
   How to Wash your Produce 37
Juicing in a Hurry 39
Coconut Turmeric Recovery 41
Alkaline Hydration 42
Gut Calming Juice 43
Cucumber Hangover Handler 44
3 Karat Immunity 45
Skin Care you Drink 46
Salty Red Carrot 47
All in the Family Energy Detox 48
Heavy Duty Detox 49
Prevent Defense 50
Greens & Grapefruit 51
Healthy Spicy Tomato Juice 52

Brainy Green Immune Boost	53
Sweet Potato Pineapple	54
Ms. Healthy	55
Juicy Omega 3	56
Facelift in a Glass	57
Blackcurrant Blood Pressure Relief	58
Insomnia Relief	59
Common Cold Zapper	60
Multivitamin in a Glass	61
Live Long and Prosper	62
Cholesterol Control	63
Tasty Veggie Detox	64
Bladder Infection Fighter	65
Kale & Broccoli Detox	66
Minty Digestive Ease	67
Dandelion Diuretic	68
The George Clooney	69
Tropical Enzyme Explosion	70
Coffee 2.0	71
V9 Juice	72
Women's Health Tonic	73
Healthy Ginger Ale	74
Cholesterol Corrector	75
Green Juice Phase One	76
Vitamin C Booster Juice	77
Immunity Mechanic	78
Iron Woman	79
Blood Sugar Balance	80
Healthy Heart	82
Shake the Cold - Warming Juice	83
Red Dandelion for the Liver	84
Breakfast with Benefits	85
Protein Building Juice	86
Better than Milk	87
Hot & Spicy Energy	88
Rehydration Juice	89

- Ulcer Relief 90
- Headache Relief 91
- Parasite & Candida Detox Juice 92
- Brain Detox Juice 93
- Ginseng Concentration Improver 94
- IQ Booster 95
- Cilantro Cholesterol Reduction 96
- Nut Milk 97
- Cilantro Detox 98
- Workout Booster Juice 99
- Folic Acid for Pregnancy 100
- The Big Brain Juice 101
- Master Antioxidant 102
- Chlorophyll and Carotene 103
- Citrus C Fighter 104
- Acne Fighter 105
- Iron – Anemia Aid 106
- Green Juice Depression Relief 107
- Migraine Relief Taco Juice 108
- Liver Cleanse in a Glass 109
- Inflammation Reducer 110
- Cool that Fever #2 112
- Fruity Flu Remedy 113
- Flu Destroyer 114
- Green Juice for Immunity 115
- Dr. Oz's Green Juice 116
- Salad on the Run 117
- Bitter Melon Hangover Handler 118
- Martha Stewart's Green Juice 119
- Jennifer Aniston's Green Juice 120
- This Juice Changed my Life 121
- The Magic Shot – Wheatgrass Juice 123
- Menu of Juices by Category 125
    - Inflammation Reduction – Anti-Aging .. 125
    - Digestion System Aids 126
    - Hangover 126

- Immune System Boosters 126
- Healthy Skin 127
- Overall Health Improvement 127
- Energy Drinks 128
- Detox Juices 128
- Cancer Fighters 129
- Lower Cholesterol & Hearth Health 129
- Weight Loss 130
- Mood, Memory, Alertness & Intelligence 130
- Blood Pressure 130
- Insomnia & Sleep 130
- Headaches, Colds, Flu & Fever 130
- Bone Health & Osteoporosis 131
- Bladder, Kidney & Liver 131
- Sex Organs / Aphrodisiac 132
- Celebrity Juices 132

References 134

Introduction

Like almost everybody, I knew intuitively that drinking fresh juice was good for me, but it wasn't until 2010, when facing a serious illness called Chronic Fatigue Syndrome (CFS), that I really saw the power of fresh juice to make a major transformation in my overall health.

On my quest for wellness, I ended up at the Hippocrates Health Institute (HHI) in Florida. At HHI, they welcome a wide variety of guests; everyone from high-performance professional athletes, to famous movie to people who have been diagnosed with Multiple Sclerosis (MS) or stage 4 cancer.

HHI has a 50 year track record of helping people improve their lives and recover from serious illness and the first thing they do with everyone who attends: start them drinking 32 ounces of green juice every day!

For me, it has been almost three years now since I had my first green juice and I bet I haven't missed more than five days in total in those three years. The effects on my health have been remarkable. Not only has my physical health been restored, but I have more mental energy, clarity and focus, and best of all, I am more optimistic and happy.

What I am presenting here is a love of juicing and a love of the health benefits that can come from taking in nutrients in a pure and concentrated form that makes them readily available to help our bodies.

Why Juicing?

The first and foremost reason to drink fresh juice is because it tastes fantastic!

Besides the great taste, whether it is a fruity juice full of exotic tropical flavors or the basic green juice, we also know that drinking juice is a just plain healthy thing to do.

I believe that drinking fresh juice is good for us on every level of our existence.

Juicing is Better than Vitamin Pills

Juicing provides nutrients to your body in an easily accessible form. In my previous book (Fart Free Vegan), I studied the digestive system and how our body breaks down food into molecules that it can then use for energy, or to fight illness or build or repair cells.

Our body uses a tremendous amount of resources converting each fork-full of food that you put into your mouth into a liquid with particles small enough that the digestive system can put them into use.

Fresh raw juice, bypasses almost all of those labor-intensive sections of the digestive system. It allows us to introduce nutrients into our body in an efficient and concentrated form.

I drink two sixteen ounce glasses of green juice every day. In order to make that much juice I wash and prepare a huge bowl of sprouts, kale, cucumber, chard, celery and anything else that I can get my hands on that looks healthy and green. That big bowl contains a vast amount of nutrition, but there is just no way in the world that I could consume that amount of green veggies every single day. I would be eating all day long, and I'd be bored out of my mind!

Juicing allows me to mainline the benefits of all those healthy foods by condensing them down into a drink that I love; that is refreshing, delicious and provides a boost of energy. More importantly I feel very good about myself just for making the choice to do something that healthy for my body.

Green Juice

My primary, go-to juice is green juice. In my mind, the greener it is, the more beneficial it is for my health. It's not to say that the other juices I have presented in this book aren't healthy, they are, but if you are not experiencing optimal health, start with green juices to get you back on track.

Green vegetables contain something called chlorophyll. Chlorophyll is extremely close in chemical composition to the hemoglobin in human blood. The extreme similarity between the green chlorophyll in plants and the red hemoglobin in human blood allows the chlorophyll to act as a powerful blood cleanser and builder.

Bringing chlorophyll into our system is like receiving a mini transfusion; refreshing and increasing red blood cell count by bringing oxygen to our cells. This oxygen provides a massive boost to our immune system because disease promoting bacteria (including cancer cells) cannot thrive in an oxygen-rich body.

Protein in Juice?

Because I'm a vegan, I often get asked, "Where do you get your protein?"

If I'm feeling a bit devilish, I'll snipe back, "The same place as the animal that you eat gets it from."

It is a fact that many vegetables have a protein content that is comparable to meat, and the protein is in a more available form and doesn't come with all the bad fats.

I'm not here evangelizing a vegan diet, merely pointing out another major benefit of juicing, especially with leafy green veggies is the energy from easy to digest protein sources. Meat provides a lot of energy, but requires a lot of energy for the body to digest, but green juice energy takes much less effort for the body to extract the benefits.

Juicing for Weight Loss

How to Achieve Permanent Weight Loss

The mistake that most people who are trying to lose weight make is that they focus all of their efforts and attention on trying to reduce their food intake which doesn't work because this is usually the area where they have the least control.

When I wanted to change my diet, I realized that I was addicted to many of the foods that I needed to get out of my diet. Using my willpower to try and force myself not to eat these unhealthy foods just put me on a roller coaster of dieting and then bingeing. Unless this is your first time trying to lose weight, I'm sure you'll recognize the pattern.

To achieve permanent change in your body, be it health improvement or weight loss (they are really the same thing), then we have to get off of the roller coaster diet trap of focusing on what we shouldn't eat, or trying to control our eating.

Real weight loss (and health improvement) comes from three things: eating high-nutrition foods, getting adequate exercise and having a positive mental attitude. I needed to work on all three of these areas before I was able to make real and permanent progress on my health goals.

Juicing is a way to provide concentrated doses of very high nutrition food that is easily assimilated by our body. It is the fastlane for taking care of that aspect of weight loss, but it must be combined with regular exercise and conscious effort to release negative thinking and replace them with positive and optimistic self images and feelings.

Juicing for Weight Loss

Some people will shed some weight on a low calorie diet; but they will lose more weight and it will be more permanent on a low fructose/low sugar diet. For maximum weight loss and health benefits getting the excess sugar out of our diet is crucial. Unfortunately this includes fructose or sugar from fruit.

Make sure you read the section that is coming up about sugar in fruit as it will make the case for why even fruit sugars need to be avoided for weight loss. That is why almost all the vegetable juice recipes in this book have an apple free option. Try and eliminate or reduce sweet fruits in your juices. Surprisingly your taste buds will adjust and you will find even the greenest, green juice to be plenty sweet.

Fibre and Weight Loss

Dietary fibre intake has been shown to promote weight loss as it increases the feeling of being full and promotes better elimination of toxins.

However juice contains only soluble fibre which is a type of fibre that is dissolved into the liquid. The real fibre in the vegetables is pulp that we are removing from the vegetables.

If you are doing a juice fast, or even replacing a meal each day to lose weight, then consider using some psyllium husks. You can add a bit to your juice to give it a smoothie texture, or just add a spoonful to water. I have been using psyllium husks for years and really like the improved elimination that they can facilitate. Make sure you drink extra water when taking psyllium.

Juice Fasting

Juice fasting is a way to speed up healing since it relieves the body of the burden of digesting food, but still provides a lot of nutrients and calories needed to normal functioning. I recommend doing some research before you embark on any kind of juice fast beyond what I'm about to mention in this section.

At Hippocrates (HHI) we were taught a type of juice fasting that has actually become quite popular now under the name of: Intermittent Fasting. Intermittent Fasting (IF) has a few elements to it, but the essence is to give the digestive system a break so that our body can divert energy and resources to healing, detox and repair work.

At HHI, we practiced two types of IF that both work together really effectively.

Daily Juice Fasting

The goal here it to give the body small breaks every day. In order to do this we didn't eat any solid foods after 6 or 7pm. This allows the stomach to clear before we going to sleep and this lets our body devote its energy to restorative processes during this rest time. In the morning, we had a shot of wheatgrass upon rising. At about 9am they served a glass of cucumber juice for its alkalizing benefits, and then at 11am we were given 16 ounces of fresh green juice. The first solid food of the day is taking sometime around 1pm.

This routine allows our body to go 16 to 18 hours every day without having to digest any new solid food, yet still provides it with all the nutrients to have energy and function at a normal level.

Weekly Juice Fasting

Besides the daily fasting at HHI, we also did a weekly juice fast every Wednesday. We would eat a normal dinner on Tuesday evening and then have green juice in place of lunch and dinner on Wednesday and then juice, as normal on Thursday morning and back to a regular lunch on Thursday at about 1pm.

This would mean going from Tuesday evening to Thursday lunch with only green juice, cucumber juice and wheatgrass shots.

If you're like me and this is the first time you've ever considered a juice fast, the idea of going without food for that long probably seems extremely unpleasant or even impossible.

Surprisingly, though it is very enjoyable. Once you can make a commitment to do it, and it needs to be a solid decision, then you can really reap the benefits. It is actually a very pleasant relief just to be free from thinking about food for a day. Sometimes I will make all the juice I need first thing on Wednesday morning and then I am "free" until Thursday lunch.

The other thing that may surprise you with these mini-fasts is that your energy actually goes up. I am able to exercise and often feel better than when I am eating. This boost is especially true of my mood and mental energy.

Done on a regular basis these short juice fasts can make a big difference in terms of weight loss and overall health. As I mentioned, please consult a health professional and do more research before embarking on any longer fasts. If you experience any symptoms like unusual headaches, nausea or anything else unusual, even when on one of these mini-fasts, don't be a hero, take some food and/or go seek medical assistance.

Juicing Precautions

Fruit Sugar – A Concern

In terms of calories and its affect on the body, sugar in the form of fruit is not much different that white sugar found in junk food. Obviously, there are a lot of healthy nutrients in fruit that do benefit the body, that are not found in junk food, but if you want to lose weight or improve your health; you will need to reduce sugar in all forms, including fruits.

Hearing someone say that you should avoid fruit is probably making you angry; just like I got angry when I first heard this.

Fruit is healthy right?

Not so fast. The fact is that fruit trees, bushes and vines, since the time that they became products (and not just growing in the wild), have been selectively bread to produce sweeter and sweeter fruit.

The reason? The sweeter the fruit, the better it sells.

"...present day fruits much sweeter than they should be, with higher amounts of sugar, resulting in higher amounts of blood sugar increases when consumed. As a result, your body must release a larger amount of insulin to bring your blood sugar back down to normal levels. The increased sucrose makes you crave more fruit (or worse-off, more sucrose-containing foods like sweets)." ~ The Caveman Doctor.com

This quote explains the other problem with too much sweet fruit; it can stimulate a normal body craving for more sugar.

For this reason, I have made fruit optional on almost all of the veggie juice recipes in this book. If you want to lose weight or are facing any kind of health challenge, focus on detoxifying, and leave out the apples and other fruits as much as possible (even carrots and beets can be high in sugar, so don't go overboard on them either). I went without fruit, or any other sugar, for over two years while I was recovering from chronic fatigue (stevia saved my life)!

Food Combining & How to Drink Juice

I wrote an entire book about food combining and how the digestive system processes food (Fart Free Vegan). It is actually quite an important topic that makes a big impact on what nutrients we absorb in our foods. While the book is primarily about solid foods, there are some important rules that do apply to juicing that will help you derive the most benefit from the healthy liquids you are drinking.

#1 "Chew" your Juice

Most people don't realize that digestion starts in the mouth. Juice, just like solid foods, needs to be mixed with the enzymes that are in your saliva in order to be properly digested. Therefore, you need to chew (the jaw action releases the saliva) even when you are drinking juice. It takes time, at least

30 seconds or a minute, with the juice in your mouth for the enzymes to be mixed thoroughly. Don't chug your juice!

#2 Food Combining in your Juice

In general, when eating solid foods, you never want to eat fruits, especially sweet fruits like apples, with vegetables. The reason for this is that fruits digest more rapidly than vegetables, so if they are mixed together and consumed at the same time, the vegetable digestion takes longer and slows down the fruit digestion. This causes gas from fermentation as the fruits "wait" for the vegetables to digest.

With juicing, what I've noticed is that for some people there isn't a negative effect from combining fruits and veggies, and for others, they have a strong reaction. Juice in general digests very quickly and easily (which is why it is so beneficial) so there may not be enough of a difference, for some people, between the digestive times of fruits and vegetables to cause a problem. The key is to pay attention to your body as you are drinking and for up to an hour afterwards to see how you are feeling. If you experience any type of reaction then make a mental note.

A reaction could be gas or bloating to discomfort or pain in the stomach after your juice. If you do have any of these symptoms after your juice, then try it next time without combining fruit and vegetables in the same juice and make sure you are sipping your juice slowly and "chewing" it well.

If you know you have a health challenge or a weak digestive system, you'll want to avoid putting any fruits (with the exception of lemon and lime) into any vegetable juices.

#3 Drink Juice on an Empty Stomach

As I mentioned in the previous section, one of the primary benefits of drinking juice is that it digests quickly and easily; more nutrients for less work for your body.

Because of this, we must drink juice on an empty stomach. The best way to understand why is with an example. Imagine a single-lane, one way street (that's what your digestive system is). There are two vehicles; one is a big truck loaded with heavy stones and the other is a Ferrari. The road is two miles long. If the Ferrari goes down the road first, there will be no problems, the truck can leave 5 minutes after the Ferrari and will never catch up.

But if the truck (solid food) enters the road first, then the Ferrari (juice) must wait until the truck is almost at the end of the road before leaving, or else he will catch the truck and be really, really frustrated (fermentation) at having to go so slowly.

The question is then, how long do you have to wait after a meal to drink your juice. Ideally, you would do like I do and have at least one glass of juice on an empty stomach first thing in the morning.

The best time for a second glass of juice is late afternoon about an hour before supper. In my past unhealthy life, this was always coffee time for me, so now I have replaced the coffee ritual with green juice. The answer to how long to wait after lunch before having your juice depends on what you eat for lunch. If you have a green salad and light dressing, then two hours may be enough, but if you have meat with a starch (hamburger and fries for example) then you may need to wait four hours or more before you stomach is sufficiently empty for the fast moving juice.

If you really want to have juice and you know you still have solid food in your stomach, then just make sure you chew it really well and sip it slowly. This will help reduce the potential for an unpleasant reaction. Just because your stomach is empty, or you had a snack, don't skip your juice, you'll still get a lot of nutrients from it.

Juicing for Kids

Kids will naturally love any type of juice. The only real precaution is that fruit juices can be quite intense for delicate digestive system.

Start by diluting your juices, maybe 50/50 with water.

Teach your child to "chew" their juice, by showing them how you do it.

Lastly, check in with them to make sure they are not experiencing any discomfort after drinking pure juice. Some juices, especially fruit juices, can be acidic and painful in the stomach. For example, as a child I always had stomach pain after drinking apple juice.

Diluting, chewing and sipping rather than gulping, will all make it easier for your kids to enjoy their juice.

Juicing Equipment

There are a lot of different opinions about what's the best type of juicer. You can actually make yourself crazy trying to sort it out, so I'll keep it simple and tell you what I was taught and what works for me.

Centrifugal or Masticating?

There are really only two types of juicers. The first are the centrifugal type juicers which are more common and typically less expensive. These juicers have a sharp blade that creates juice using a cutting action with high speed and force.

The second are the masticating juicers which have an auger or gear system that turns slowly and grinds or presses the juice out of the produce.

Since the primary benefit that we want from our juice is living nutrients and enzymes, a high speed centrifuge type juicer will generate heat and not give the same quality juice as a slow speed masticating juicer.

Masticating juicers crush the veggies slowly much in the same way that our teeth do. It makes sense to me, whenever possible to emulate nature with our food.

That said, I think the difference between the two types of juicers is not extreme. Certainly, drinking juice from a centrifuge juicer is 100 times better than not having any fresh juice at all. If you have a centrifuge juicer and can't afford to upgrade to a masticating juicer, then you are fine; start juicing!

But, if you are considering buying a juicer then there is one other consideration in the centrifuge versus masticating debate that is worth considering; masticating juicers handle greens and leafy vegetables a lot easier and more effectively than centrifugal juicers.

Centrifuge juicers are great at solid mass fruits and vegetables like carrots, sweet potatoes, apples etc, but they don't tend to do a good job with the leafy greens that are so important for healthy juicing. There are workarounds, like wrapping leafy greens around or between harder veggies, so the cause is not completely lost, but if you are going to buy a new juicer and you want to regularly add sprouts or leafy greens to your juice, you will be much better off with a masticating juicer.

Clean up Time

One other really important factor when buying a juicer is the time it takes to clean it. We all have busy lives and for most people it isn't easy to find extra time, even for something a healthy as juicing. The fact is that some juicers take longer to clean than it takes to make your juice.

When I first started using an Omega Vert, it took so long to clean, and was such a hassle fiddling with all the little parts, that I found I was not making my juice everyday because it felt like too much work (although it does have very high yields). I knew this was not the right juicer for me. You'll want to get a juicer that is super easy to clean so it doesn't provide you with a mental drain towards making juice.

Recommended Juicer Models

If you do decide to buy a **centrifugal juicer**, one of the best on the market is the Breville BJE510XL. I know some people who are very serious about making juice and they swear by this machine.

Masticating Juicers

I have personal experience with all of the following juicers, so I can give you the pros and cons of each.

Healthy Juicer GP27

This is a hand-crank manual juicer that you can buy on Amazon for about $50. When I first started juicing, I had a centrifugal juicer and wanted to try a masticating juicer. I was low on funds and didn't know if I would actually like it, so I bought one of these since it was so reasonable.

I actually used this juicer for almost 6 months and made 32 ounces of juice a day with it.

Pros: inexpensive, and you get a decent arm workout cranking the veggies through it! It also has a Zen element to make your juice manually; I would watch uplifting videos on YouTube while I made my juice. The Zen element is why I took so long to upgrade to a powered masticating juicer.

Never underestimate the mental, emotional and physical health benefits of slowing down and doing things the old-fashioned way in our fast-paced modern world.

It is light and portable enough that you can take it traveling with you.

Cons: very time consuming. It took me 20 to 30 minutes to crank through enough veggies for my 32 ounces of juice each day (not including veggie prep time). Pulp comes out quite wet, so it isn't getting the maximum juice from your veggies.

It can also be a bit fragile. I did break the handle once because I was trying to feed too much produce into the auger at once.

Green Star

The Green Star is a top of the line masticating juicer. It is very heavy duty. You can basically just jam almost any type of fruit or veggie into it and it will keep on cranking out the juice. It sells on Amazon for about $470.

Pros: very solid and durable. It produces very dry pulp. Of all the juicers I have used; it gets the most juice yield from your produce.

Cons: high price and the worst part of this juicer for me, it is quite a bit of work to clean.

If you want "the best" and have the extra time to clean it, or you leave it out and make juice several times a day, this is probably the juicer for you.

Juicing Recipe Cabinet

Omega 8006

This is my favorite juicer and the one I currently own and most often recommend.

Pros: it is very simple and fast to clean. It takes me less than 3 minutes if I clean. Reasonably priced at about $270. Fantastic support; I broke one of the pieces and when I told them I used my juicer every day, the company FedEx'd a replacement part to me overnight at no cost to me. It comes with a "blank" that can be used to make pates, ice creams and nut butters (won't be like store bought, but still they are fresh and pretty good). This added feature is a huge bonus with this juicer.

Cons: it's plastic so it can be a bit fragile. I have found you have to be careful putting wheatgrass into it (not too much at a time as it can knot up and crack the auger cover). Pulp is not quite as dry as on Green Star, but still really good.

Overall, this is a great juicer. I have used mine everyday for over 2 years and I love it a lot.

Other Tools

You may want to have a citrus juicer, I just use a manual one which saves me having to fire up and then wash my main juicer if I am just making orange, grapefruit or lemon juice.

A blender is also essential for a couple recipes in this book and most people will already have one. If you want to get into the power blender game, I have an alternative to the expensive Vitamix, called an OminBlend V which is about 2/3rds of the price and almost the same strength (I have owned both).

But to be totally honest, about 95% of the time I use my $30 Magic Bullet for blending all the recipes in this book that use bananas or need blending.

How to Buy Your Produce

As I mentioned previously, I prepare of a massive bowl of produce that I juice every day. I make sure that it is almost all certified organic. If it isn't organic, I am buying it from a local farmer that I trust. The reason is that if I am putting that much produce into my body to get condensed nutrients; I will also be condensing any pesticides or fertilizers that are present in the foods as well.

11 Foods you Must Buy Organic

There are some non-organic foods that are worse than others. The following is a list of foods that you should never juice (or use at all) if they aren't certified organic:

- Potatoes – often contain residue of pesticides even after they are washed.

- Celery – has no skin to provide a layer of resistance to sprayed pesticides. Any health benefits of "conventional" celery will be off-set by the toxic chemicals that you don't be able to wash off.

- Apples – apples are very susceptible to pests, therefore farmers have to use large amount of pesticides to keep their produce protected.

- Peaches and Nectarines – According to the USDA, more than 95% of all nectarines contain toxic pesticides.

- Spinach and Lettuce – More than 80% of spinach contains pesticides and lettuce is very similar.

- Pears – The environmental working group lists pears as one of the top foods containing pesticides.

- Strawberries – over 90% of strawberries contain pesticides due to the very thin skin which absorbs any chemicals into the fruit where they cannot be washed off.

- Grapes – another fruit with a thin skin that actually absorbs the pesticides into the cells of the fruit where it can't be washed off.

- Bell Peppers –Particularly avoid peppers that may come from outside of the US and Canada where chemicals use on food are not enforced to a very high standard.

- Kale and Collard Greens – due to their large, leafy surface area, they are susceptible to containing insecticides.

- Summer Squash (zucchini and yellow squash are the most common) – also susceptible to containing insecticides even after washing.

11 Foods that are Okay, Even if they're Not Organic

There are some foods that are not really worth spending a lot more money on to purchase certified organic. Typically it is because these foods don't attract a lot of natural insects or pests, so farmers don't need to use pesticides or insecticides on them.

One tip about using non-organic fruits and vegetables: always wash the skins or peel before you cut into them, otherwise your knife will drag any pesticide residue into the part you are going to eat.

- Onions – onions are naturally antibacterial, so it makes sense that they wouldn't attract pests and therefore don't require a lot of pesticides.

- Avocados – the thick skin that we don't eat protects the fruit from any chemicals.

- Corn – a crop that uses a lot of fertilizer to produce, but the kernels should be free of chemicals. Now the moral issue of supporting this type of farming, that's a different subject. I've included corn on this list because it won't have a lot of chemicals in it, but corn is heavily genetically modified. Some studies claim that it is virtually impossible to find corn that isn't GMO. Personally I don't buy non-organic for this reason.

- Pineapple – can be okay if you are removing the skin, but if you want to put the peel into you juice, then go organic.

- Mango – another fruit that is okay because of a thick skin that we don't eat.

- Asparagus – like onions, asparagus don't have many threats from insects or predators, so very few chemicals are used when farming them.

- Peas – studies indicate that conventionally grown peas are one of the foods that contain the least amount of pesticides. Presumably the study is referring to peas that are not in the pods.

- Cabbage – another food that doesn't require much spraying to grow. Tear off the first layer of outer leaves, give it a rinse and you're good to go.

- Papaya – a fantastic fruit for making juice. Make sure you rinse the papaya and then remove the skin and you will be leaving behind almost all the pesticide residues.

- Watermelon – if you don't eat the rind, you can enjoy non-organic watermelon.

- Sweet potato – this amazing food with its surprising nutrient content, doesn't require a lot of chemicals to grow. Sometimes they are dipped in an anti-fungal chemical after they are picked. For this reason it's best to peel any non-organic sweet potatoes before juicing or eating.

Farmer's Markets

Since I've started to understand the relationship between health and food, my local farmer's market has become my favorite place to shop.

I have learned to notice the quality of my food, especially fresh produce, and the difference in quality that you can purchase from your local farmer's market and even a great health food store like Whole Foods, can be very dramatic.

The reason that fresh fruits and vegetables are so health-giving for us is that they are full of enzymes and nutrients. However, these nutrients start to die and decay the moment the produce is picked.

There is just no way that produce at Whole Foods, which if you live in Florida like I do, may come from California, or even South America, can be as fresh or healthy as it will be from a farmer that picked his produce the morning before he came to the market to sell it.

If you look closely, you'll easily see the difference. Another great benefit of the farmer's market is that you can ask the farmer about their crops. Even if they aren't certified organic, it isn't uncommon for a farmer to be chemical free, but not certified organic, just because he is small and the process of getting a farm certified as organic is expensive and laborious.

The other huge advantage at the farmer's market is variety. I juice all kinds of weird greens that I wouldn't normally eat: mustard, sweet potato tops, turnip tops, carrot tops, chards, radish tops etc. And, even better, because I've become friends will all my local farmers (I'm the "weird juicing guy"). Many of them will save greens for me and give them to me for nothing. For example most people ask the farmers to remove the carrot, radish and turnip tops. I show up at the end of the day and take home a huge bag of ultra-nutritious certified organic, juice greens for free or very low cost!

Make friends with your local farmers, it's healthy for you and for the planet.

In this highly commercialized world that we live it, it's easy to take our farmers for granted (food just comes from store shelves right?), but we won't have much left to enjoy in our lives if there isn't anyone growing high quality food to nourish us and keep us healthy.

The Real Superfood: "Live" Green Juice

As I covered in the section on how to shop for juicing ingredients, a big factor in the quality of your produce and your juice is how long it takes from the time it is picked until the moment you drink it, since produce actually starts to decay the moment it is picked (separated from its life source).

That is why at the Hippocrates Health Institute (HHI) they make their green juice primarily from "living foods" – wheatgrass and sprouted sunflowers and peas. These foods are literally harvested and, within hours, turned into juice to maintain and pass along the maximum benefits in the form of enzymes and nutrients.

There simply isn't a more healthy food on the planet than green juice made from freshly harvested sprouts, which is why for almost three years now I have sprouted my own sunflowers, peas, wheatgrass, alfalfa and others to use in my juices and salads.

Growing your Own Living Foods

Growing enough of all of the types of sprouts to use in juice requires planning, organization and time. Now that I have my systems down, I spend about 20 to 30 minutes a day on it; but it takes longer at first.

In some regions, like here in Florida, there are growers that sell and ship fresh wheatgrass and sprouts via overnight express delivery. It can be quite expensive, but if you want to try it, or you have the extra money, the health benefits are well worth adding these real superfoods to your diet. There are also fresh sunflower, pea and wheatgrass available in many Whole Foods stores. Or if you are really lucky there will be someone growing and offering these fresh sprouts for sale in your town; likely at a farmer's market.

Even though juicing with living foods will not be for everyone, I felt compelled to mention it since this is a book about juicing for health and living green juices are the Lamborghini of juices. If you are dealing with mild to serious health issues, it may very well be worth your time to begin adding these superfoods to your juice and diet.

It would take another whole book to provide a complete guide to growing wheatgrass, sunflower and pea sprouts but there are many great videos on YouTube where people share their methods. Below I will provide a quick start alternative.

My Easy Sprouting System

Wheatgrass, sunflower sprouts and pea sprouts which are the mainstays of the HHI green juice are all grown in soil and require a commitment of time, space and materials (trays, soil, ordering seeds etc) to grow properly. But there is an easier way to get started adding living sprouts to your juice.

Juicing Recipe Cabinet

When I travel, I can't take trays and soil and seeds with me, so I created an easy sprouting system. You will need the following supplies:

- Four ½ gallon clear plastic containers (the ones I use are from Nutiva brand coconut oil, but there are quite a few foods that come in appropriate containers, or you can use glass ones if you have them)

- Four squares of very small holed plastic mesh to cover the tops of the jars (you can get this at a fabric store, it comes in different colors and is used in kids' ballerina costumes)

- Four sturdy elastic bands to hold the mesh on the tops of the jars

- Three tablespoons of Alfalfa seeds per jar (you can experiment with other small seeds like: clover and radish or many sprouting stores sell excellent blends. I don't recommend broccoli as it can be very difficult to grow)

- A rack or other system that will hold the jars upside down at a 45 degree angle and allow water to drain out of the jars after rinsing without forming a puddle that is touching the jar. An old dish rack is perfect, but small bowls that elevate the mouth of the jar off of the bottom of the bowl will work as well (remember to drain the run-off water out of the bowls each time you rinse the sprouts, or it will begin to smell)

Day one we are going to just start one jar, then on day two we will start the next one and day three the third one etc. Our goal is to have one jar of fresh sprouts available each day and since it typically takes four days for the sprouts to be ready we have four jars. If your sprouts take longer, you will need to do more jars to have a continuous supply.

Step 1: Put three tablespoons of alfalfa seeds into one jar and put the mesh on the top with the elastic.

Step 2: Rinse and drain the seeds a couple times to wash the seeds.

Step 3: Fill the jar about half full with water and let sit 8 to 12 hours. I like to let it sit overnight.

Step 4: The next morning, drain the water and rinse the seeds. Place jar upside down on your rack.

Step 5: Rinse the seeds three times a day (morning, mid-day and evening) and place upside down on rack.

Step 6: When the seeds start getting about ½ an inch long, or on about day three, move the jars near a window to allow the sprouts to green up before harvesting.

Step 7: Harvest, by pulling off the mesh and washing the sprouts really well. I use a salad spinner. You can fill your salad spinner (or a large bowl) with water and put the sprouts in. The seed husks will float to the top and you can scoop most of them out by hand. (Of course if you are using your sprouts for juice, you can save time and just leave the husks as they are okay to put into your juicer.) Shake the sprouts around in the water to give them a good cleaning, then spin or squeeze the sprouts to remove the excess water. If you have Ziploc bags with the micro-holes in them, or "green bags" you can store this sprouts for 3 or 4 days in the fridge, but I recommend using them immediately in your juice!

Do my Sprouts have Mold?

I remember when I first started sprouting like this how disappointed I was to find fuzzy white mold on my sprouts. I consulted an expert and was told to look really carefully, up close, at my sprouts. Actually, what I thought was mold was actually tiny white fibers on the root of each alfalfa sprout. These tiny fibers are seeking moisture. 99% of the time with these types of small sprouts, what looks like mold, will actually be a signal that it is time for watering.

Super-Juice Ready

Now you can try adding in these amazing living sprouts to you juice recipes. With the exception of the recipes that are all fruit, try adding some of these sprouts to any other juice in this book for a powerful boost of living enzymes and minerals.

When I'm sprouting like this, I "drink" about one jar of these sprouts a day. Of course you can add them to your salads and sandwiches as well.

If you get hooked on these sprouts and want to take it to the next level, or you just want to skip ahead to try the full-on soil sprouting with sunflowers and peas, get in touch (JonSymons.com/Contact/) and I'll be happy to send you some information.

While not quite as nutrient and protein rich as sunflowers or peas, these small sprouts pack a big punch of living vitality and energy that you'll never get from store-bought juice ingredients. I highly recommend that you try this simple and easy way to add them to your juice.

Juicing Recipe Cabinet

Prepare your Produce for Juicing

Measuring & Proportions

With juice it's difficult to measure portions since raw foods can vary so much. One cucumber can be vastly different size from another one, same goes for celery stalks or even lemons. If you want to have the perfect tasting juice, you'll need to plan for this fact and sip your juice as you create it. Since the intention of this book is primarily medicinal, I don't sweat the flavor too much. Personally I've consumed juice with some pretty weird flavors, but my health did improve!

I've tried to measure out the ingredients of each juice to provide one portion or slightly more, but as I mentioned, it can vary a lot depending on the actually ingredients you use. My motto is to always make extra, and in the worse case, store it and use it later.

Peals, Skins & Rinds

The peals, skins and rinds of some fruits and vegetables contain a lot of nutrients, but they may have a slightly bitter taste. If you are buying organic produce and you can handle the flavor, leave them on.

If you are using citrus fruits (lemons, limes, oranges or grapefruits) and the peel is too bitter (it is full of good nutrients) at least try and use the pith from under the rind and put that through your juicer as it contains flavinoids which can give the immune system a huge boost. Personally, I add a ½ of a lemon, including peel to almost every juice I make.

If you are using non-organic produce, you must remove the skin for everything as they will be full of pesticides and other chemicals.

How to Wash your Produce

About a year ago I was in line at my local Whole Foods and there was a gentleman in front of me asking for a refund for a couple bunches of certified organic kale that he had purchased.

"My wife asked me to return these because there were worms in it," he explained to the cashier.

I couldn't help poking my nose in a little bit to explain that the fact that there was worms in his kale was actually a good thing. It meant that the kale was actually appealing to living creatures (worms and humans), unlike non-organic vegetables.

Obviously, though, we don't want to be eating or juicing these worms. I had a girlfriend who taught me the trick for getting worms out of the most difficult organic veggies like kale or broccoli.

It just involves soaking the kale in salty water for a couple minutes. You need to make sure the entire kale leaf is underwater. The salty water makes the worms, or caterpillars very uncomfortable and they crawl out of leaves and float on the surface of the water. It only takes a couple minutes, while you are scrubbing the rest of your vegetables and then you can be sure you are getting the best of your organic produce and not adding insects to your diet.

I also recommend scrubbing veggies with a veggie wash, or my personal choice is to use Grape Seed Extract (GSE). GSE is a natural substance that kills bacteria, fungi and parasites. I have a small spray bottle that I fill with water and add about 10 drops of GSE and I use it to spray veggies before scrubbing.

Juicing in a Hurry

Having a plan for working a juicing habit into a busy lifestyle may be the most import aspect of enjoying the health benefits of juicing.

Making a juice once every two weeks will produce minimal benefits. To get the most out of it, we need to make juicing a part of our daily habits which requires some strategizing.

The biggest reason people don't juice is the time involved, so it is really important to spend as little time as possible to get your juice made. Below I've shared my tips for becoming more efficient. (See also the section on juicing equipment as the type of juicer also can make a big difference in wash-up time.)

Batching your Juice Prep

Personally, I drink 16 ounces of green juice twice a day. It just isn't realistic that I have the time for two sessions of preparing juice each day. So I make a large batch every afternoon, and store half of it until the next morning.

This saves me about 20 to 30 minutes a day because I don't have to do everything (washing, juicing and cleaning the juicer) twice.

The other way that I save time is to batch up the preparation of juicing ingredients. I can spend time and wash all the things I will need for three or four days of juicing at once, that is a big time saving as well. Then I put the clean ingredients into the fridge, wrapped in plastic, and they are ready when I need them.

Juice Storage Tips

It's best to drink your juice right after you make it, but that is not always practical.

I have a 16 ounce jar, which I fill to the rim with juice to minimize the amount of oxygen that is inside. Then I twist the lid on nice and tight. The other thing that helps keep my juice fresh is that I add lemon to almost every juice I make, which is a natural preservative and controls oxidation.

Frozen Juice

If you are really short of time, or you know you will be, you can prepare a large batch of juice and then freeze it. It will be less nutritious than fresh, but it will be a lot more nutritious than bottled juice or nothing at all.

Just as I mentioned before, add lemon to your juice and fill a container to minimize the air in the container. I would use a plastic container for freezing as juice (or any liquid) will expand when it freezes and this expansion could break a glass jar.

Canned or Bottled Juices

Best to avoid these "fast food" juices. Most of the time they will have added sugars or preservatives, they won't be made from organic fruits or veggies, and they will be heated or pasteurized will destroy virtually all of the enzymes and nutrition in the juice.

Coconut Turmeric Recovery

Recover from yoga and workouts faster by reducing inflammation and easing sore muscles.

Ingredients:

1 oz of turmeric juice, or 1 teaspoon of turmeric powder

1 cup of coconut juice

As an alternative to coconut juice you can mix the turmeric juice or powder into any green drink, like the "Light Green Snap" juice (celery, cucumber, ginger and lemon).

Directions:

If using fresh turmeric (you can order it fresh from Amazon now!), run it through your juicer and pour it into either your coconut or green juice.
If you are using powdered turmeric, you'll need to blend gently or shake the powder into your juice.

In Cabinet Under:

Cold or flu relief, anti-inflammatory (arthritis), anti-bacterial, antioxidants that fight cancer causing free radicals

Alkaline Hydration

This juice is a great all-around health tonic. Celery has natural sodium (a salty taste without any of the harmful effects of salt) so it is a perfect drink if you are dehydrated or for a hot day.

Ingredients:

- 4 large celery stalks
- 1 medium cucumber
- ½ of a lemon (including peel if you want the full benefit)

Directions:

Wash and run ingredients through juicer. Lemon peel will make the juice creamy and slightly bitter, but it has many health benefits.

In Cabinet Under:

Aides digestive system inflammation, hydrating, anti-cancer – overall immune booster, helps with insomnia due to high magnesium levels, balances body pH levels.

Gut Calming Juice

All of the ingredients of this juice work to reduce inflammation in the digestive system, helping the body to repair damage caused by stress or eating too many acidic foods.

Ingredients:

- 1 medium cucumber
- 1 cup of mint leaves
- ½ head fennel
- ½ lemon
- ½ to 1 inch of medium thick ginger root

Directions:

Scrub the cucumber and fennel and lemon rind and rinse. Soak and rinse the mint leaves. Cut everything into juicer sized pieces and run all the ingredients through your juicer.

If you want the juice to be creamier, and can handle a bit of a bitter taste, there are a lot of nutrients in the lemon peel; so I leave it on, but you can also remove it.

Be careful with the ginger, you may want to add a bit at a time ad taste as you go, or the juice will be too "hot."

In the Cabinet Under:

Aids digestive system inflammation.

Cucumber Hangover Handler

Simple cucumber juice taken before you go to sleep helps to replenish the body's electrolytes and B vitamins enough to avoid a hangover and a headache.

Great as a morning wake-up juice. At Hippocrates Health Institute guests are served cucumber juice as breakfast every morning.

Ingredients:

 1 or more large cucumbers

Directions:

Wash cucumber, slice and run through juicer.

In the Cabinet Under:

Helps with hangover, balances acidity because cucumber is very alkaline, aids high blood pressure due to potassium and magnesium, aids detoxification due to high water content

3 Karat Immunity

This simple carrot and pepper juice boosts immune system with beta-carotene and antioxidants. The peppers supply huge amounts of vitamin C. One glass of this juice and you'll sparkle.

Ingredients:

3 carrots

2 red or 1 red and 1 yellow bell pepper

Directions:

Wash the carrots (don't peel) and the pepper, slice into smaller pieces if needed, and run through juicer.

In the Cabinet Under:

Beta-carotene, vitamin C, vitamin A, immune boost, antioxidant.

Skin Care you Drink

Supporting beautiful skin from the inside out, this juice features our 3 Karat Immunity juice's carrots and pepper with added sweet potato and broccoli, both of which boost the anti-inflammatory properties of this juice.

Ingredients:

- 3 carrots
- 1 medium red bell pepper
- ½ of a sweet potato
- 1 large broccoli spear

Directions:

Wash carrots, pepper and sweet potato by scrubbing with a brush. Soak broccoli in salty or Grape Seed Extract water for 5 minutes and then rinse. Cut sweet potato into slices or chunks and then run all the veggies through the juicer.

In the Cabinet Under:

Beta-carotene, vitamin C, vitamin A, vitamin K, immune boost, antioxidant, blood sugar balancing (sweet potato reduces sweet cravings and provides long lasting energy).

Salty Red Carrot

This beautiful orange red juice is a general health tonic because of its balance and wide range of nutrients.

Ingredients:

- 2 large celery sticks
- 3 medium carrots
- 1 medium beet
- ½ of a lime (peel optional if organic)

Directions:

Scrub and wash the lime, beet and carrots, leaving the peel. Wash the celery. Chop the beet so that it will fit and run everything through the juicer. If you're brave and want the extra (a lot!) of nutrients in the lime peel try adding that as well.

In the Cabinet Under:

Vitality and general healthy booster.

All in the Family Energy Detox

A combination of cucumber and melon which are from the same food family create a sweet and refreshing energy juice with detox qualities.

Ingredients:

1 medium cucumber
½ cantaloupe or other melon (peeled)
1 pear
Small bunch of fresh mint

Directions:

Scrub cucumber and pear. Peel cantaloupe and discard peel. Rinse the mint. Slice cantaloupe and cucumber so they will fit and run everything through your juicer.

In the Cabinet Under:

Cantaloupe is proven to be effective in the prevention of metabolic syndrome. This juice provides protein and carbs for energy and anti-inflammatory nutrients for body detox.

Heavy Duty Detox

Three all-stars in job of detoxification; all together in one juice. The pears contain phytonutrients including flavonols that have been shown to reduce chronic inflammation and oxidative stress which is at the root of many diseases.

Ingredients:

- 2 pears, with skins
- 3 stalks of celery
- 8 broccoli spears

Directions:

Scrub the pears and celery to clean. Soak the broccoli in salty water to clean. Cut them all to fit and run them through the juicer. Stir and sip slowly.

In the Cabinet Under:

Detox, anti-aging and anti-inflammatory.

Prevent Defense

This juice features the kale, the supermarket's least sexy superfood. You can pretend you're suffering with this juice, drinking it only because you want to be healthy, but actually with the carrot and orange balancing the kale, it tastes fantastic. There are more phytonutrients in the peel and white pulp of oranges than in the juicy orange center, so you them as well if want to get maximum nutrition and can handle a bit of bitterness.

Ingredients:

3 carrots

1 orange remove the peel (too bitter), but keep some of the pith (white stuff) if possible.

5 large kale leaves

Directions:

Soak the kale in salty water and rinse. Scrub the carrots and cut the orange into juicer sized pieces. Run them through your juicer.

In the Cabinet Under:

Vitamin C, immune booster, lowers bad cholesterol, anti-inflammatory.

Greens & Grapefruit

Grapefruits, especially the peels, have been widely used as an aid for weight loss. Combine them with the three other power greens in this juice and you also have a great juice for detox and vitality.

Ingredients:

- 1 grapefruit, with peel if organic
- 2 cups of spinach
- 4 large kale leaves
- 2 sticks of celery

Directions:

Soak the kale and spinach in salty water. Scrub the celery and the grapefruit. Cut the grapefruit into pieces that will fit and then run everything through your juicer.

In the Cabinet Under:

Weight loss, detox, and energy.

Healthy Spicy Tomato Juice

Parsley is a great source of volatile oils that have been proven to help neutralize some carcinogens and inhibit tumors, especially in the lungs. Tomatoes are rich in vitamin C and vitamin A and are full of healthy phytonutrients.

Ingredients:

- 1 bunch of parsley
- 1 lemon, including skin if organic
- 5 tomatoes
- 1 clove of garlic peeled (optional)

Directions:

Soak the parsley and rinse. Scrub the lemon, if using the peel, and the tomatoes. Cut tomatoes and lemon into juicer sized pieces. Run all ingredients through the juicer.

In the Cabinet Under:

Cancer fighter, immune booster and antioxidant.

Brainy Green Immune Boost

This juice is a powerful immune booster – with some serious carotene on the side. Increased carotene has been linked to improved cognitive function.

Ingredients:

- 3 large kale leaves
- 1 cup of spinach leaves
- 1 carrot
- 1 grapefruit, including peel, or part of peel if organic

Directions:

Scrub and rinse the carrot and grapefruit. Soak the spinach and kale in salty water. Cut grapefruit and kale and carrot if necessary to juicer sized pieces. Run all of them through the juicer.

In the Cabinet Under:

Immune support, carotene, brain food.

Sweet Potato Pineapple

This unique juice harvests the wonderful flavor and healing properties of the sweet potato and combines it with the digestive enzymes of the pineapple and the immune support of the carrot. Sweet potatoes, unlike regular potatoes, can actually regulate blood sugar providing a stable source of energy.

Ingredients:

½ of a pineapple (peeled)

1 medium large sweet potato with peel if organic

1 carrot

Directions:

Scrub and rinse the sweet potato and carrot. Cut all ingredients into small enough pieces and run through juicer.

In the Cabinet Under:

Immune support, energy booster and digestive system aid.

Ms. Healthy

This juice is not going to win any beauty contests; unless there is a prize for Ms. Healthy. A juice for detoxifying with nutrients from the kale and tomatoes and for immune support with vitamins from the lime and beet. It comes out a bit brown, thus the name, but the juice is surprisingly tasty.

Ingredients:

- 4 large kale leaves
- 5 tomatoes
- 1 beet
- 1 lime including peel if organic

Directions:

Scrub and rinse tomatoes, beet and lime. Soak kale in salty water and rinse. Chop into pieces small enough to run through juicer and then juice all the ingredients.

In the Cabinet Under:

Detoxification, immune support, bone health, cardiovascular support and anti-cancer support.

Juicy Omega 3

The omega-3 essential fatty acid in flax seeds support healthy joint functions and muscle development. By using flax seeds rather than flax oil, you will also obtain the laxative (from the fiber) and the anti-cancer properties that aren't found in flax oil.

Ingredients:

- 3 sticks of celery
- ½ of a pineapple
- ½ to 1 inch of ginger
- 2 tablespoons of flax seeds (soaked) or 1 tablespoon of flax oil

Directions:

Add flax seeds to ½ cup of water in a covered container. After 15 minutes shake vigorously. Seeds should be suspended in a think clear liquid. Allow flax seeds to soak for least 3 more hours. Scrub celery and ginger and rinse. Cut peels off of pineapple. Run them all, through your juicer. If you are using flax seeds (liquid and all – put don't add more water) into a blender and blend into a thick creamy paste. Then add juice and blend it all together. It should be almost a smoothie texture. If you are using flax oil, then just stir or shake it into your juice before drinking.

In the Cabinet Under:

Anti-cancer, laxative, omega-3, joint and muscle support, digestive enzymes and gut support.

Facelift in a Glass

This salad in a glass juice is a tonic for healthy skin, promoting cleansing from the inside out. In a scientific study 10 of 11 women experienced visible improvements to their skin and 7 or of 11 saw an improvement in wrinkles by eating watercress.

Ingredients:

- 3 stalks of celery
- 3 tomatoes
- Small bunch of parsley
- Small bunch of watercress
- ½ lemon, with peel if organic

Directions:

Scrub celery, tomatoes and lemon if using peel. Soak and rinse parsley and watercress. Chop lemon and tomato into pieces that will fit in juicer. Run them all through the juicer.

In the Cabinet Under:

Watercress, as well as a skin tonic contains more vitamin C than oranges, as well as high amounts of vitamin A and beta-carotene.

Blackcurrant Blood Pressure Relief

Studies indicate that the oil from black currants can regulate blood pressure. It is also a very powerful antioxidant.

Ingredients:

½ cup fresh blackcurrants
4 sticks celery
½ inch ginger
1 apple (optional)

Directions:

Soak blackcurrants in grape seed extract or veggie scrub and rinse. Wash celery and ginger and apple. Cut apple into juicer sized pieces and run all the ingredients through the juicer.

In the Cabinet Under:

Blood pressure support and strong antioxidant.

Insomnia Relief

There's a substance by the name of lactur carium in lettuce that sedates the nervous system and promotes sleep.

Ingredients:

1 head of romaine lettuce
½ lemon, including peel if desired
2 apples

Directions:

Soak and rinse lettuce. Scrub lemon and apples. Chop lemon and apples so they fit in juicer. Run them all through the juicer.

In the Cabinet Under:

Insomnia relief.

Common Cold Zapper

This juice features a massive dose of vitamin C, the warming effect of ginger and the bug fighting antibacterial and antiviral effects of garlic.

Ingredients:

- 2 grapefruits, peel included if organic
- 1 inch of ginger root
- 1 lemon, peel included if organic
- 1 clove of garlic

Directions:

Scrub and rinse the grapefruits, ginger and lemon. Chop into pieces that will fit in juicer. Feed them all through your juicer including garlic.

In the Cabinet Under:

Lower blood pressure, antibacterial and antiviral, relief from common cold.

Multivitamin in a Glass

Great for growing kids and women at risk for osteoporosis due to the nutrients phloridzin and boron that are found in apples. This juice is also rich in many other nutrients. Think of it as a multivitamin in a glass.

Ingredients:

- 3 leaves of kale
- 2 leaves of collard
- ½ cup of parsley
- 2 carrots
- ½ red bell pepper
- 2 apples

Directions:

Soak the kale, collard and parsley in salty water or veggie wash for 5 minutes, then rinse. Scrub carrots, pepper and apples. Chop into pieces that will fit in juicer and run everything through your juicer.

In the Cabinet Under:

Bone health support, vitamin A, vitamin C, vitamin E, Magnesium, Potassium, Folic Acid and Vitamin B6.

Live Long and Prosper

This juice is very high in carotenes which have been linked to longer life expectancies. If you enjoy your life, and want more of it, drink this juice on a regular basis. Carotene is also great at protecting against sunburn, so having a glass of this juice before any sun exposure may help avoid sun damage to your skin.

Ingredients:

- 1 medium beet, including tops if possible
- ½ medium sized sweet potato
- 3 carrots

Directions:

Scrub and rinse all three root vegetables. If you are using the beet tops, or the carrot tops, soak and rinse. Cut everything into juicer-sized pieces and run through your juicer.

In the Cabinet Under:

Longevity, sunburn protection, carotene, vitamin A, vitamin C.

Cholesterol Control

Contains a healthy dose of foods known to lower bad cholesterol: garlic, ginger and peppers.

Ingredients:

¼ inch slice of ginger

1 clove of garlic

4 carrots

½ cup parsley

½ to 1 pepper (the ideal is a pepper that contains capsicum: jalapeños, Hungarian wax pepper or even bell peppers all fit the bill).

Directions:

Scrub the ginger, carrots and pepper and then rinse. Soak and rinse parsley. Chop everything into juicer sized pieces and run through your juicer.

In the Cabinet Under:

Lower cholesterol, vitamin A, vitamin C.

Tasty Veggie Detox

5 simple ingredients that you probably already have in your fridge that are packed with nutrients and antioxidants to turbo-charge detoxification.

Ingredients:

4 carrots

2 sticks of celery

½ medium beet, with tops if possible

½ cup of parsley

1 apple (optional – for sweetness)

Directions:

Soak and rinse the parsley. Scrub and rinse the carrots, celery, beet and apple. Cut everything up to fit into your juicer and run them all through. Stir and sip slowly.

In the Cabinet Under:

Detoxification, antioxidant, vitamin A, vitamin C, vitamin E.

Bladder Infection Fighter

Cranberries are proven to fight bladder infections. If it is not the fall season, you can find frozen and thaw them out before juicing. If it is fall and you have extra freezer space, consider stocking up (right after Thanksgiving or Christmas when they go on sale) and freeze some of these healthy berries to use year-round. This juice includes apple and orange to offset the bitter taste of the cranberries, but if you want the maximum benefits of the cranberries, use as more cranberries and less and orange. This is because the sugar in the sweet fruits can actually promote the bacteria that are causing the infection.

Ingredients:

1 cup of cranberries (use more if you are omitting or reducing the apples and oranges)

2 medium apples

1 orange (peeled, but keep pith if possible)

Directions:

Soak and rinse cranberries. Scrub the apple and peel the orange. Cut apple and oranges up and run everything through your juicer.

In the Cabinet Under:

Bladder infection relief, vitamin C.

Kale & Broccoli Detox

The cabbage family of veggies, including kale and broccoli, have the ability to detox heavy metals from the body and to help the immune system fight cancer causing cells.

Ingredients:

- 4 large kale leaves
- 2 medium broccoli spears
- ½ of a head of cabbage
- 2 carrots
- 2 apples (to taste)

Directions:

Soak kale, broccoli and cabbage in salty water, then rinse. Scrub carrots and apples (if using). Slice them all into juicer sized pieces and run them all through your juicer.

In the Cabinet Under:

Detox – heavy metals, fight cancer causing cells.

Minty Digestive Ease

This juice loads you up with digestive enzymes (bromelin) from the pineapple. Ginger has been an all natural way to relieve motion sickness, gas, nausea, morning sickness and loss of appetite for hundreds of years. Kiwi fruit has been linked to improved digestion and relief from bloating and the feeling of being over-full. And mint is an effective way to ease spasms in the intestines. This juice is multi-dimensional digestive tract support.

Ingredients:

- ¼ inch of ginger
- ¼ cup of fresh mint leaves
- 1 kiwi fruit, including skin
- ¼ pineapple

Directions:

Rinse mint leaves. Peel the pineapple. Scrub the kiwi and ginger gently. Slice the pineapple and kiwi so they'll fit into your juicer. Run all the ingredients through your juicer. Stir and sip slowly.

In the Cabinet Under:

Digestive enzymes, relief from: intestinal spasms, bloating, motion sickness, gas, nausea, morning sickness and loss of appetite.

Dandelion Diuretic

Dandelion leaves can be used as a diuretic, to aid the body in getting rid of too much fluid by increasing urine production. They are also known to stimulate the appetite and aid digestion. Celery is also a diuretic and it rehydrates and alkalizes the body, helping it to return to an optimal pH level.

Ingredients:

- 2 stalks of celery
- 1 bunch (about 3 cups) of fresh dandelion leaves
- 3 carrots

Directions:

Scrub carrots and celery. Soak dandelion leaves in salty water and rinse. Slice carrots if needed so they fit in the juicer. Run all the ingredients through the juicer.

In the Cabinet Under:

Promotes production of urine (diuretic), hydration, and alkalization.

The George Clooney

If you're a guy you want to be him, and if you're a woman you want to be with him; either way this juice will help. Garlic and arugula have been used as aphrodisiacs for 2000 years. Hot chili pepper will get the blood flowing to all the right areas of the body. Make sure to drink with your partner, so you both have the romantic flavor of garlic on your breath.

Ingredients:

- 3 cups arugula
- 2 cups parsley
- 1 small clove of garlic
- 1 chili pepper
- ¼ of a pineapple

Directions:

Peel pineapple and cut into chunks that will fit in your blender. Soak and rinse arugula and parsley. Scrub pepper and remove seeds. Run all the ingredients, through juicer... save the pepper and garlic until last, small pieces at the time, stirring and sipping your juice, until the flavor is how you like it.

In the Cabinet Under:

Aphrodisiac.

Tropical Enzyme Explosion

This is a perfect breakfast juice. Wake your digestive system with tropical fruits that are loaded with healthy enzymes. As well the orange peel and pith contain anti-cancer agents and hesperidin which can lower blood pressure.

Ingredients:

½ mango (peeled)

2 oranges (use a bit of peel if they are organic)

½ papaya (peeled)

¼ pineapple (peeled)

1 banana (optional)

Directions:

Peel mango, papaya and pineapple. Wash the oranges and peel off any peel that you won't be using; try and use the pith as it is loaded with nutrients. Slice everything into juicer sized pieces and run it all through the juicer. If you want to make it into a smoothie, put the juice into a blender and add the banana and blend.

In the Cabinet Under:

Enzymes, digestive aid, lower blood pressure and anti-cancer.

Coffee 2.0

Leave behind the acid stomach, the dehydration, headaches and short term energy from coffee with this powerful carroty green blast in your mornings. Sip this juice slowly to spread out the energy from the sweet carrots.

Ingredients:

- 1 large handful of parsley
- 5 or 6 medium carrots

Directions:

Soak and rinse parsley. Scrub and rinse the carrots. Slice carrots if needed to get them into the juicer. Run both ingredients through your juicer.

In the Cabinet Under:

Energy, coffee replacement.

V9 Juice

Nine nutritious summer veggies that make an amazing juice.

Ingredients:

1 bunch of spinach

1 stalk of celery

3 carrots

3 or 4 radishes (include some of the leaves if they are organic and very fresh)

½ a medium cucumber

1 tomato

1 broccoli spear

½ red bell pepper

Directions:

Soak spinach, radish tops, and broccoli and then rinse. Scrub celery, carrots, cucumber, tomato and pepper. Chop and slice everything so it fits into your juicer, and run them all through.

In the Cabinet Under:

Vitality, overall health improvement, immune support.

Women's Health Tonic

Fennel and celery both contain phytoestrogens. Phytoestrogens have been shown to modulate hormone related diseases in women and they are used for the treatment and prevention of breast cancer.

Ingredients:

- 1 small fennel bulb including leaves and stems
- 2 celery stalks
- 2 apples (optional – add cucumber or more celery if omitting)

Directions:

Soak and rinse the fennel leaves and stalk. Scrub the celery and apples. Slice everything to fit your blender, and run it through.

In the Cabinet Under:

Breast cancer, PMS, menopause.

Healthy Ginger Ale

When I was a kid and I had stomach ache, my Mom gave me ginger ale, but these days I wouldn't drink or give my kids sugary sodas. This juice is so goods kids and adults will prefer it to anything that comes in a plastic bottle or can.

Ingredients:

¼" slice of ginger (or more to taste)
slice of a lemon peel removed
1 green apple (e.g. Granny Smith)
¼ cup of water or sparking mineral water

Directions:

Scrub the apple and slice into pieces that will fit into juicer. Run lemon and apple through juicer, then ginger to taste. Mix in mineral water and serve.

In the Cabinet Under:

Stomach or digestive pain relief. Soda pop replacement for kids.

Cholesterol Corrector

The ingredients in this juice are packed with beta carotene and plant sterols which help to lower bad cholesterol.

Ingredients:

- ¼" slice of ginger (or more to taste)
- 1 apple including peel
- 4 carrots

Directions:

Scrub carrots and apple and cut into juicer-sized pieces. Run all the pieces through your juicer, and adjust flavor with ginger.

In the Cabinet Under:

Cholesterol control.

Green Juice Phase One

To me, "green juice" is about the healthiest phrase in the English language. Juices loaded with green vegetables support the foundations of our health in the most efficient possible way. Green juices are many magnitudes more valuable to the body that taking supplements. The apple is primarily for people who need their juice to be sweet, leave it out if you can and add cucumber or celery.

Ingredients:

- 1 large handful of parsley or wheatgrass
- 2 large kale leaves
- 1 large handful of spinach leaves
- 1 or 2 apples (optional – can be replaced with cucumber or celery)

Directions:

Soak parsley, kale and spinach in salty water or veggie wash, then rinse. Scrub apples and cut into juicer sized pieces. Run them all through the juicer. Sip slowly and "chew" the juice to mix with your saliva before swallowing to get the maximum benefit.

In the Cabinet Under:

Immune system support, overall vitality and health boost.

Vitamin C Booster Juice

This will come as a surprise to many, but the veggies in this juice contain a lot more vitamin C than the citrus fruits that people normally think of as a source for vitamin C.

Ingredients:

1 medium broccoli spear

1 red bell pepper

1 yellow bell pepper

2 apples (optional – can be replaced with cucumber or celery)

Directions:

Soak the broccoli in salt water or veggie scrub and then rinse. Scrub the peppers and apples. Cut everything up into juicer sized pieces and run through your juicer.

In the Cabinet Under:

Vitamin C and immune system boost.

Immunity Mechanic

This juice contains many nutrients proven to aid the immune system in its job of fighting off disease in our body. This juice also has flavinoids and other antiviral and antioxidants to help ward off and overcome illness.

Ingredients:

1 orange (use peel if the flavor is acceptable to you – it contains more nutrients than the juicy part of the orange)

½ pineapple with skin

½ to 1 cup strawberries (with greens, they are full of nutrients as well)

1 banana (without peel)

Directions:

Scrub the orange and rinse. Rinse the pineapple and strawberries. Slice and cut the orange and the pineapple so that it fits into the juicer. Run the orange, pineapple and strawberries through the juicer. (You may want to separate the orange from its peel and only run a little bit of the peel at time into your juice. Orange peel can be an intense flavor and we don't want to overwhelm the rest of the juice.) Then pour the juicer into your blender and blend in the banana.

In the Cabinet Under:

Immunity, antiviral, and antioxidant.

Iron Woman

The juice is high in iron and is especially good for women who may be susceptible to anemia or low iron levels. Having enough iron is essential to energy and healthy blood.

Ingredients:

- 1 medium beet with tops
- 1 large kale leaves
- 1 broccoli spear
- 4 carrots
- 1 apple (optional for sweetness – can be replaced with cucumber or celery or lettuce)

Directions:

Soak kale, broccoli and beet tops in salty water, then rinse. Scrub beet, carrots and apple. Cut or slice everything into pieces that will fit into juicer. Run everything through your juicer.

In the Cabinet Under:

Iron booster.

Blood Sugar Balance

This juice features the Jerusalem artichoke or sunchoke. Jerusalem artichokes aren't really artichokes; they look more like ginger, and have a mild starchy flesh. They make a good potato replacement if you are on a low starch or diabetic diet. In this juice the Jerusalem artichoke supplies inulin which is different than other starches in that it actually helps keep your blood sugar level stable, rather than causing spikes in blood sugar that are common with other starches like potato or processed grains. Inulin also supports the digestive tract by feeding the healthy bacteria in your gut.

Ingredients:

- 2 cloves of garlic
- ¼" of ginger
- 1 handful of parsley
- 4 carrots
- 1 cup of Jerusalem artichokes

Directions:

Scrub carrots, ginger and Jerusalem artichokes. Soak and rinse parsley. Cut everything into pieces that will fit into your juicer and run them all through.

In the Cabinet Under:

Blood sugar balancer, energy stabilizer and supports healthy intestinal flora.

Blood Sugar Balancer Take 2

Our previous blood sugar balancing juice featured inulin-rich Jerusalem artichokes. Version two introduces jicama; another uncommon juice ingredient that is equally rich in the nutrient inulin. Like the Jerusalem artichoke, jicama also promotes healthy bacteria in the digestive tract and reduces inflammation.

Ingredients:

- 1, 2 or more inches of jicama
- 4 medium carrots
- 1 apple, optional (substitute cucumber or celery for less sweetness)

Directions:

Scrub jicama, carrots and apple and rinse. Cut into juicer-sized pieces and run them all through your juicer.

In the Cabinet Under:

Energy, blood sugar balance: hypoglycemia, diabetes (avoid the apple and less carrots), immune booster, intestinal flora balancer.

Healthy Heart

This juice is delicious and low in calories, if you are juicing for weight loss. Leave the rind on the cantaloupe and leave the tops on your strawberries as it saves prep time and adds extra nutrition. Cantaloupe has vitamins and nutrients that are beneficial for your heart and will boost your immune system.

Ingredients:

- ½ cantaloupe with rind
- 1 cup strawberries with greens

Directions:

Soak the strawberries in veggie wash and rinse. Scrub cantaloupe and rinse. Chop cantaloupe into juicer size pieces. Run cantaloupe and berries through the juicer.

In the Cabinet Under:

Healthy heart, immune system.

Shake the Cold - Warming Juice

Even if you drink it cold, this is a naturally warming juice that will promote perspiration and flush out your cold before it can get a hold of you. If you really need to kick a cold, add a clove of garlic.

Ingredients:

- 1 inch of ginger root
- ¼ lemon with peel
- ½ clove of garlic (optional)
- 1 cup of hot water, or cold water

Directions:

Scrub lemon and ginger and rinse. Chop into pieces that will fit and run everything through your juicer.

In the Cabinet Under:

Cold relief.

Red Dandelion for the Liver

Many people consider the common dandelion a miracle food, especially when it comes to liver health. It contains so many health improving nutrients that its Latin name actually means, "official remedy for disorders."

Ingredients:

I large fresh dandelion root including greens if possible

½ medium beet, including the tops if possible

2 carrots

1 apple, optional (use cucumber or celery for less sweetness)

Directions:

Soak dandelion tops and beet tops and rinse. Scrub beet and dandelion roots and carrot and apple then rinse. Cut everything into pieces that will fit and then run them all through your juicer.

In the Cabinet Under:

Improves any liver related conditions, general health and vitality.

Breakfast with Benefits

This tropical blueberry smoothie is a perfect breakfast juice. Slow
carbs to give you energy throughout the day and the antioxidants from the blueberries are actually proven to boost your brain health and improve your memory. A perfect breakfast that is quick to prepare. Sip during your commute as you listen to brain boosting meditation music.

Ingredients:

¼ pineapple, including rind

1 to 1½ cups of blueberries

l banana

Directions:

Soak the blueberries in veggie wash and rinse. Scrub rind of pineapple and rinse. Chop pineapple into pieces that will fit in juicer. Run pineapple and blueberries through your juicer. Pour juice into blender, add banana and blend quickly until smooth.

In the Cabinet Under:

Mental focus, memory, brain health.

Protein Building Juice

This juice is very rich in potassium which provides tools for the body to build proteins and build muscle. It also helps with the metabolism of carbohydrates and overall body growth. Perfect juice for growing kids and anyone working out.

Ingredients:

- 4 carrots
- 1 large handful of fresh parsley
- 1 large handful of spinach
- 2 celery stalks
- 1 tomato

Directions:

Scrub carrots, celery and tomatoes and then rinse. Soak parsley and spinach in veggie wash or salty water and rinse. Cut everything into pieces that fit and run all the ingredients through the juicer.

In the Cabinet Under:

Protein, potassium, muscle building, overall body growth.

Better than Milk

This juice has a comparable amount of calcium to a glass of milk, without any of the hassles of climbing under a cow! You'll also receive a wealth of other beneficial nutrients without the lactose that causes allergies in so many people.

Ingredients:

½ head of red cabbage (use green if red isn't available)

2 large kale leaves

1 red bell pepper

2 apples, optional (use cucumber or celery for less sweetness)

Directions:

Soak cabbage and kale in salty water or veggie wash, then rinse. Scrub red pepper and apples and rinse. Cut everything into pieces that will fit and then run it all into the juicer. Sip slowly and enjoy the healthy juice!

In the Cabinet Under:

Calcium, building strong bones, relaxing, regulates heartbeat.

Hot & Spicy Energy

The natural heat in this juice is perfect to get your blood pumping, generating body heat and providing a boost of energy. It also has a detoxifying effect.

Ingredients:

2 or 3 radishes, add some radish greens if they are still fresh

1 red or yellow pepper

2 tomatoes

Piece of hot pepper to taste (jalapeño, so similar hot pepper)

Directions:

Scrub the radishes and soak the leaves if you are using them. Scrub the peppers and tomatoes. Cut everything into small pieces and run them all through the juicer. Put hot pepper in last in small pieces so you can adjust "heat" of your juice.

In the Cabinet Under:

Improve circulation, energy drink, heat generation, and detoxification.

Rehydration Juice

This juice provides an excellent way to replace electrolytes for athletes. It's also great on hot sweaty days or for anyone feeling weak. This juice is also very nutrient dense, so it provides protein and many other health benefits. This juice is hearty enough to be used as a meal replacement.

Ingredients:

- 1 handful of parsley
- 1 handful of spinach
- 2 carrots
- 2 tomatoes
- 2 stalks of celery
- ½ cucumber with skin
- ½ bell pepper

Directions:

Soak parsley and spinach in veggie wash or salty water. Scrub carrots, tomatoes, celery, cucumber and pepper. Cut non-leafy veggies into juicer sized pieces. Feed everything into juicer. Sip slowly and enjoy!

In the Cabinet Under:

Rehydration, meal replacement juice, overall nutrition and vitality.

Ulcer Relief

Cabbage is wonderful soother for any kind of stomach discomfort.

Ingredients:

- 2 cups of green cabbage (about ¼ of a cabbage)
- 2 tomatoes
- 4 stalks of celery

Directions:

Soak the cabbage in salty water then rinse. Scrub the tomatoes and celery. Cut everything into juicer-sized pieces and run through your juicer.

In the Cabinet Under:

Ulcer relief.

Headache Relief

Persistent or repeating headaches can be a sign of deeper health problems. For me, I had headaches every few days or two years before my chronic fatigue set in; so consult a professional if this rings true for you. The potassium and magnesium that are found in this juice can bring relief.

Ingredients:

- 5 large kale leaves
- 1 cucumber
- 4 stalks of celery
- 1 lemon, with rind if possible
- 1 to 2 inches of ginger
- 1 or 2 Granny Smith apples, optional (for sweetness only, if you want it less sweet, use extra cucumber or celery)

Directions:

Soak the kale leaves in salty water and rinse. Scrub cucumber, celery, lemon, ginger and apples. Cut everything into pieces that will fit and run everything through your juicer.

In the Cabinet Under:

Headache relief.

Parasite & Candida Detox Juice

Many people, if not most people, will benefit from a parasite and Candida detoxification. In this juice, the nutrients include FOS (fructo-oligosaccharides), which provides food for the healthy bacteria in your digestive system. The tomato, lemon and the cucumber help to balance the pH level of your digestive tract, which promotes the healthy bacteria and inhibits the unhealthy ones. And garlic is a strong antimicrobial. If you want to take this juice to the next level, sprinkle some acidophilus or probiotic powder to your juice.

Ingredients:

- 2 tomatoes
- 2 stalks of celery
- 1 lemon, with rind for extra nutrition
- 1 – 2 cloves of garlic
- 1 medium cucumber

Directions:

Scrub the tomatoes, celery, lemon and cucumber and rinse. Cut everything into juicer-sized pieces and run them all through the juicer along with the garlic to taste.

In the Cabinet Under:

Parasite, yeast, fungus detox. Long-term energy improvement.

Brain Detox Juice

The ingredients in this juice are proven sources of malic acid. Malic acid has been shown to remove aluminum from the brain, which is thought to be a major contributor to Alzheimer's disease.

Ingredients:

- 1½ cups of grapes, without stems
- 1 apple with skin
- 1 cup of strawberries, with greens and stem on

Directions:

Soak grapes and strawberries in veggie wash and rinse. Scrub apple and rinse. Chop apple down and run everything through your juicer. Stir and sip slowly.

In the Cabinet Under:

Brain power, detox, and memory improvement.

Ginseng Concentration Improver

The secret ingredient in this juice is ginseng which has been used for centuries as a brain food. If you can't get fresh ginseng, there are ginseng powders that can be used as a substitute.

Ingredients:

- 1 cup strawberries, with greens and stem on
- 1 or 2 peaches, pitted
- 1 apple with peel
- 1 tablespoon of fresh ginseng

Directions:

Scrub ginseng, peaches and apple. Soak and rinse strawberries. Remove pits from peaches. Cut everything into juicer-sized pieces and run all ingredients through the juicer. Sip slowly.

In the Cabinet Under:

Brain power improvement, mental clarity, improved attention.

IQ Booster

Coenzyme Q10 is an enzyme that brings many benefits to the brain. And the spinach in this juice is an excellent source of coenzyme Q10, which is also aided in boosting brain power by the hot pepper which supplies vitamin C.

Ingredients:

   1 large or 2 smaller tomatoes, including skin
   1 bunch of spinach
   3 stalks of celery
   ½ bulb of fennel, including stalks and leaves
   1 clove of garlic
   1 jalapeño pepper, or cayenne pepper powder

Directions:

Scrub tomatoes, celery, jalapeño and fennel bulb and then rinse. Soak spinach and fennel tops. Cut everything into juicer-sized pieces and run it all through the juicer.

In the Cabinet Under:

Brain improver, concentration, neuron enhancer.

Cilantro Cholesterol Reduction

The cilantro in this juice is proven to reduce LDL (bad cholesterol) levels. It is also an aid to heavy metal detoxification and contains antioxidants which protect your body from free radicals which cause aging.

Ingredients:

¼" slice of ginger (or more to taste)

4 carrots

1 bunch of cilantro, stems and leaves

Directions:

Scrub and rinse the carrots and ginger. Cut carrots down so they will fit into your juicer. Soak and rinse the cilantro. Run all the pieces through your juicer, and adjust flavor with ginger.

In the Cabinet Under:

Cholesterol reduction, detox and anti-aging.

Nut Milk

Nut milk is not really a juice, but I couldn't help including a recipe here just because it is such a good and healthy alternative to dairy milk. Personally I would never combine it with fruit or vegetable juice, but some people do with okay results. If you have any discomfort or indigestion from using almonds, after you soak them, leave them an extra day to "sprout" (make sure you rinse them every couple hours). If that doesn't improve the digestion, then substitute sunflowers; they are easier to digest.

Ingredients:

- 1 cup soaked raw organic almonds (or sunflower seeds)
- 2 cups pure water
- Vanilla, optional – to taste
- Stevia, optional – to taste

Directions:

Soak sunflower seeds or almonds overnight in 6 cups of water. Rinse well and drain the next morning. Put seeds or almonds and water into high-speed blender and blend thoroughly. Strain out the pulp (almond pulp makes a great skin scrub). Stir in vanilla and stevia and enjoy.

In the Cabinet Under:

High protein, energy.

Cilantro Detox

This is a variation of my "Kale & Broccoli Detox" juice. Kale and broccoli have the ability to remove heavy metals from the body and to help the immune system fight cancer causing cells. Here we add in some cilantro for a fresh flavor and to boost up the heavy metal detoxification and anti-aging antioxidant quality of this juice.

Ingredients:

    4 large kale leaves

    2 medium broccoli spears

    ½ of a head of cabbage

    1 bunch of cilantro, stems and leaves

    2 apples (to taste)

Directions:

Soak kale, broccoli, cilantro and cabbage in salty water, then rinse. Scrub apples and rinse (if using). Slice everything into juicer sized pieces and run them all through your juicer.

In the Cabinet Under:

Detox – heavy metals, fight cancer causing cells and anti-aging.

Workout Booster Juice

Pre or post workout the ingredients in this juice boost electrolytes for athletes. Post workout this juice provides protein for muscle repair and growth. A hearty juice it can be also be used as a meal replacement. The cilantro adds potassium, which is a mineral that keeps fluid levels balanced in the body, helping you remain hydrated. I take this juice with me and sip on it during my workouts.

Ingredients:

- 1 handful each of parsley, spinach and cilantro
- 2 carrots
- 2 tomatoes
- 2 stalks of celery
- ½ cucumber with skin
- ½ red bell pepper

Directions:

Soak parsley, cilantro and spinach in veggie wash or salty water. Scrub carrots, tomatoes, celery, cucumber and pepper. Cut non-leafy veggies into juicer sized pieces. Feed everything into juicer. Sip slowly and enjoy before, after or during your workout.

In the Cabinet Under:

Rehydration, meal replacement juice, overall nutrition and vitality.

Folic Acid for Pregnancy

Besides being like a multivitamin in a glass, when we add the avocado to this recipe, it makes a creamy, delicious texture that is high in folic acid – great for pregnant or wanting to be pregnant women.

Ingredients:

 5 leaves of kale or collard

 ½ cup of parsley

 2 carrots

 ½ red bell pepper

 2 apples (optional – can be replaced with cucumber or celery)

 1 avocado

Directions:

Soak the kale, collard and parsley in salty water for 5 minutes, then rinse. Scrub carrots, pepper and apples. Chop into pieces that will fit in juicer and run everything through your juicer. After juicing, use a blender to gently mix in avocado. Just blend until smooth as over-blending can destroy nutrients in your juice.

In the Cabinet Under:

Folic Acid for pregnancy support and many vitamins and minerals for overall health.

The Big Brain Juice

For optimal function our brains need good fats in the form of essential fatty acids or Omega-3. In the book *Change Your Brain, Change Your Life,* author Dr. Daniel G. Amen considers avocado one of the top brain-health foods. The kale and chard in this recipe also contain essential fatty acids to power your brain.

Ingredients:

- 6 large kale or chard leaves
- 1 medium broccoli stem and floret
- 1 large cucumber
- 1 handful of spinach
- 2 celery stalks
- ¼ pineapple (optional for flavor and/or sweetness)
- 1 avocado

Directions:

Soak kale/chard, broccoli and spinach in salt water or veggie wash and rinse. Scrub avocado, pineapple, celery and cucumber. Chop them all small enough to run through juicer. Peel the avocado. Put everything except avocado through juicer. Blend juice and avocado gently – just enough to create a smooth texture.

In the Cabinet Under:

Improve brain health and cognitive functioning.

Master Antioxidant

My nickname for this juice is "everything but the kitchen sink" antioxidant. Parsley and tomato both contain important antioxidants that prevent premature aging and many degenerative diseases. Then we add in the avocado which is one of the few foods that contain the master antioxidant glutathione which benefits the nervous system, liver and our immune system.

Ingredients:

- 1 bunch of parsley
- 2 medium tomatoes
- 1 medium cucumber
- 3 stalks of celery
- 1 red bell pepper
- 1 avocado

Directions:

Soak and rinse parsley. Scrub and rinse tomatoes, cucumber, celery and pepper. Rinse the skin of avocado, peel, remove pit and set aside. Cut everything but the avocado into pieces the will fit into your juicer. Run everything but avocado through your juicer. Add juice and avocado into blender and blend gently.

In the Cabinet Under:

Antioxidant, anti-aging, degenerative disease prevention and immune boost.

Chlorophyll and Carotene

The antioxidant qualities, which prevent oxygen-based cell damage, in parsley and tomatoes give this juice its healthy punch. As well, studies have shown that the carotene and chlorophyll in spinach slow down cancerous cell division in several types of cancer.

Ingredients:

- 1 large handful of spinach
- 1 bunch of parsley
- 2 medium tomatoes
- 1 medium cucumber
- 3 stalks of celery
- 1 red bell pepper

Directions:

Soak and rinse spinach and parsley. Scrub and rinse tomatoes, cucumber, celery and pepper. Cut everything into pieces that will fit and run everything through your juicer.

In the Cabinet Under:

Antioxidant, anti-cancer, and immune booster.

Citrus C Fighter

Ginger is a powerful antioxidant that combats some types of cancer cells and helps slow tumor growth. High vitamin C in citrus fruits protect cells from oxidant damage.

Ingredients:

- 2 inches of ginger
- 1 grapefruit
- 2 limes
- 1 cup of cranberries
- 2 oranges

Directions:

Scrub and rinse all the fruit and ginger. There is a benefit to leaving the peals on any of the citrus, but it can result in more bitter juice. Try just adding the lime peels if you are not used to the flavor. Cut them all ingredients into juicer sized pieces and run through your juicer (I prefer to put my citrus into a regular juicer as opposed to a citrus juicer, for better extraction and I like to include the peels and pith).

In the Cabinet Under:

Cancer prevention, antioxidant and high Vitamin C.

Acne Fighter

This sweet and simple juice is high in vitamin C and nutrients which provide the skin with vital nutrients. Carrots also aid in detoxifying the liver, which is the source of many skin problems, including acne. This juice is very sweet, so sip it slowly to avoid a blood sugar spike and resulting crash.

Ingredients:

- 4 medium carrots
- 2 oranges (peeled, but try and leave the white pith under the peel as it has many healthy nutrients)
- 2 apples

Directions:

Scrub the oranges, apples and carrots. Cut them all into pieces that will fit in you juicer and run them all through.

In the Cabinet Under:

Anti acne, healthy skin, liver detox and high vitamin C.

Iron – Anemia Aid

The tomato has a splendid combination of iron and vitamin C which promotes the formation of new red blood cells which helps to restore the body from anemia. Beets and their tops just look like they would be high in iron, and in fact they are.

Ingredients:

- 1 medium beet with tops
- 2 tomatoes or 3 to 4 plum tomatoes
- 1 carrot
- 1 handful of parsley
- 1 small hot chili pepper (optional – but really beneficial)
- 2 celery stalks
- 5 or 6 radishes (use the greens as well if they are organic and still looking fresh)

Directions:

Soak beet tops, parsley and radish tops and rinse. Scrub beet, tomatoes, carrot, celery and radishes and rinse. Cut or slice everything into pieces that will fit into juicer. Run everything through your juicer.

In the Cabinet Under:

Iron booster, anemia restoration.

Green Juice Depression Relief

As someone who has suffered from depression, I can say first hand that a large part of this illness is related to the food we eat and our physical health. The lemon in this juice contains potassium which controls blood pressure and aids in reducing mental stress and depression. The spinach contains magnesium which, if it is deficient in the body, reduces levels of serotonin which is a neurotransmitter essential to a feeling of well being and many other brain functions.

Ingredients:

- 3 celery stalks
- 3 cups of spinach
- 3 leaves of kale
- 1 small lemon (leave peel on for maximum nutrition)
- 1 apple – optional (use granny smith for less sweetness and more nutrition)

Directions:

Soak spinach and kale leaves, and then rinse. Scrub celery, lemon and apple and rinse. Cut everything into pieces that will fit in juicer and run them all into your juicer. Sip and chew slowly.

In the Cabinet Under:

Depression relief, mood and brain booster.

Migraine Relief Taco Juice

The capsaicin in bell and cayenne pepper blocks pain transmission and it also effective in relieving migraines and regular headaches. If you like Mexican flavors, you will love this juice any time.

Ingredients:

- 1 stalk of celery
- 1 handful of cilantro
- ½ clove of garlic
- 1 large bell pepper
- 1 scallion or a 3 or 4 green onions
- 1 regular or 4 or 5 cherry tomatoes
- Dash of cayenne pepper spice

Directions:

Soak cilantro and rinse. Scrub celery, pepper and tomatoes and rinse. Cut everything to size and run through your juicer. Stir or shake in the cayenne pepper to taste and sip slowly.

In the Cabinet Under:

Headache and migraine relief.

Liver Cleanse in a Glass

Arguably the liver is the most important organ in the body in terms of affecting our overall health. Without a clean and healthy liver, your digestive system will not function properly and you will not have abundant energy. The leafy greens, garlic and turmeric all provide a massive boost to the liver and aid in its detox.

Ingredients:

1 to 2 inches of fresh turmeric (or ½ teaspoon dried)

1 beet with tops (the tops are essential in this recipe)

1 to 2 cups of spinach leaves

1 clove of garlic

2 medium carrots (with tops if possible)

3 celery stalks

Directions:

Soak beet tops, spinach, and carrot tops in salt water or veggie wash and then rinse. Scrub turmeric, beet, carrots and celery and then rinse. Cut to size and run them all through your juicer. Stir and sip slowly.

In the Cabinet Under:

Liver detox and cleanse. Overall health booster.

Inflammation Reducer

Chronic inflammation has been linked to high blood pressure, infections (viral and bacterial), arthritis, heart disease and candida. This juice helps fight inflammation by boosting the immune system and providing anti-inflammatory nutrients. Don't forget to also get regular exercise, as that is also one of best weapons against inflammation.

Ingredients:

- 3 large broccoli florets (use the stem of the broccoli as well)
- 3 cups of spinach leaves
- 1 medium sweet potato
- 1 inch of ginger root
- 2 inches of turmeric root
- 1 large cucumber
- 4 or 5 celery stalks

Directions:

Scrub and rinse sweet potato, ginger, turmeric, celery and cucumber. Soak broccoli and spinach leaves in veggie wash or sea salt, then rinse. Cut into pieces and run them all through your juicer. Stir and sip slowly.

In the Cabinet Under:

Anti-inflammation. Helps with: high blood pressure, infections (viral and bacterial), arthritis, heart disease and candida.

Cool that Fever Juice #1

Lemon juice actually increases the body's ability to perspire which is essential to overcome a fever. Pear juice has a cooling effect on the body as well. The beet and carrot replenish nutrients that your immune system needs to fight the infection.

Ingredients:

- 1 beet with tops
- 3 medium carrots
- 1 lemon with rind
- 2 medium pears

Directions:

Scrub the beet, carrots, lemon and pears and then rinse. Soak and rinse the beet tops and carrot tops (if available). Cut everything to size and run through your juicer. Stir and sip slowly.

In the Cabinet Under:

Fever and cold or flu relief.

Cool that Fever #2

Another fever-reliever juice, this one is fruitier and lighter tasting; likely more appealing for kids. If serving to a child, dilute with at least 25% water, so they don't have a big sugar hit from the natural sugars in the fruit.

Ingredients:

- 1 sweet potato
- 2 stalks of celery
- 2 medium pears
- 2 medium apples (a less sweet variety, like Granny Smith)

Directions:

Scrub all the ingredients and then rinse. Cut into juicer-sized pieces and run through your juicer. Stir and sip slowly.

In the Cabinet Under:

Fever relief, or just general cooling on a hot day.

Fruity Flu Remedy

Flu symptoms are the result of your body's immune system fighting an infection. This juice is not a hard core flu fighter, but it tastes great and the vitamin C in the strawberries does provide a gentle boost to the immune system. We leave the tops on the strawberries as they also provide nutritional benefits.

Ingredients:

- 6 stalks of celery
- ½ of a lime
- 3 cups of strawberries (leave the tops on)
- 1 apple

Directions:

Scrub the celery and apple and rinse. Rinse the lime and the strawberries. Cut into pieces and run everything into your juicer. Stir and sip slowly.

In the Cabinet Under:

Flu relief.

Flu Destroyer

This juice is a serious dose of relief, and yes, when I say that, I mean I have completely abandoned taste considerations. If you want to get better faster, and you'll drink anything to make that happen, then this is the juice for you. It is a powerful immune booster and infection fighter. Make sure if you add the full amount of garlic to this juice, you sip it slowly as garlic can be intense and burn your mouth or upset your stomach if you take too much at once. You can also chew a bit of apple peel with this juice to balance the sting of the garlic.

Ingredients:

- Up to 4 cloves of garlic
- 1 inch of ginger
- 1 lemon, including the peel
- Fresh hot pepper, or cayenne pepper spice to taste
- ½ cucumber
- 2 stalks of celery

Directions:

Scrub lemon peel, ginger, pepper, celery and cucumber and rinse. Cut everything down in size and run it all through your juicer. Stir and sip SLOWLY. This recipe doesn't make a lot of juice, it is meant more of a shipping shot drink.

In the Cabinet Under:

Flu remedy.

Green Juice for Immunity

The kale, ginger, carrots and spinach in this juice all pack a big punch of antioxidants and nutrients to supercharge your immune system and help it knock the flu out of your system. This juice is more powerful without the apple, so leave it out if you don't need the sweetness. Any type of sugar, even from fruit, should be avoided if you are sick, as it will feed the illness-causing virus or bacteria.

Ingredients:

- 2 large kale leaves
- 2 medium carrots – including tops if available
- 2 celery stalks
- ½ cucumber
- 2 cups of spinach (or any other dark leafy greens)
- ½ to 1 inch of ginger root
- ½ apple (optional for sweetness only)

Directions:

Soak the kale, carrot tops and spinach and then rinse. Scrub carrots, celery, cucumber and apple. Cut into smaller pieces and run all ingredients through your juicer.

In the Cabinet Under:

Flu relief and general immune booster.

Dr. Oz's Green Juice

Just for fun and, of course, because it's a very healthy drink, here's the green juice that Dr. Oz says he drinks every morning. It is a very healthy green juice to begin with if you are used to only very sweet and fruity drinks.

Ingredients:

- 3 stalks of celery
- 1 cucumber
- ¾ of an inch of ginger
- ½ lemon, with rind
- 1 lime, with rind
- 1 bunch of parsley
- 2 cups of spinach
- 1 or 2 apples for sweetness if needed (otherwise add more cucumber and/or celery)

Directions:

Scrub celery, cucumber, lemon, lime and apples and rinse. Soak and rinse parsley and spinach. Cut everything up and run through your juicer. Stir and enjoy.

In the Cabinet Under:

Celebrity juice, cold remedy, overall health booster and maintainer.

Salad on the Run

This juice is a great overall health booster. I will make some in the morning when I know I won't be able to get away from my desk for a proper lunch, or if I know I'm going to eat food that isn't so healthy, this juice will give my immune system a boost to balance out the bad foods. You may resist the idea of adding onion, but it is a powerful immune booster and is proven to fight bad bacteria in the body.

Ingredients:

- 1 handful of parsley
- 1 lemon, including rind
- ½ onion or 4 green onions
- 1 sweet red pepper
- 3 small tomatoes
- 1 cucumber
- 3 stalks of celery

Directions:

Soak and rinse parsley (and green onions if using them). Scrub lemon, pepper, tomatoes, cucumber and celery, then rinse. Peel the onion. Cut into pieces and run through your juicer.

In the Cabinet Under:

Anti-bacterial, anti-infection (cold or flu). Overall immune booster and health maintenance.

Bitter Melon Hangover Handler

You might wish you could, but you can't turn back the clock and let "sensible-you" manage your drinking last night, so let's get some healthy nutrients into your system and provide a boost in fighting that headache, nausea and "run over by a truck" feeling. The main ingredient is bitter melon which has been used as a medicinal food in the orient for hundreds of years. You may need to visit an oriental market to find it or in a pinch you can substitute cucumber.

Ingredients:

- 1 medium bitter melon
- ½ of a large grapefruit
- 1 lemon, with peel

Directions:

Peel the grapefruit. Scrub and rinse the bitter melon and the lemon. Cut into pieces and run through your juicer. Stir and sip slowly. This juice is bitter, but worth it!

In the Cabinet Under:

Hangover cure.

Martha Stewart's Green Juice

This is the green juice that Martha drinks to start her day. The ingredients her provide an overall health boost. Like taking a multi-vitamin, but a in a form that the body can get a lot more benefit from.

Ingredients:

- 1 stalk of celery
- 1 cucumber (peeled if not organic)
- 1 inch of ginger
- I bunch of parsley
- 1 bunch of spinach
- ½ of a medium apple
- ½ of a medium pear
- ¼ of a papaya (peel and remove seeds)

Directions:

Scrub celery, cucumber, apple and pear, and then rinse. Soak and rinse parsley and spinach. Cut everything to fit and run through your juicer. Stir and sip slowly.

In the Cabinet Under:

Celebrity juice, overall health booster and digestive aid.

Jennifer Aniston's Green Juice

Jennifer has had a long and profitable career and she attributes part of that success to her daily green juice. She has concocted a tasty blend of nutritious ingredients.

Ingredients:

- 1 cucumber
- 1 beet with tops
- 1 bunch of spinach
- 3 or 4 large kale leaves
- 1 clove of garlic
- 1 inch of ginger root
- 2 carrots with tops if possible
- 2 stalks of celery

Directions:

Soak and then rinse beet tops, spinach, kale and carrot tops. Scrub and then rinse cucumber, ginger, carrots and celery. Cut everything down to fit and run it all through your juicer.

In the Cabinet Under:

Celebrity juice, overall health booster.

This Juice Changed my Life

This is the green juice recipe that they serve twice a day at the Hippocrates Health Institute (HHI). It is high protein, alkalizing and full of vital, immune-boosting, nutrients. As soon as I made this juice part of my daily routine, my three-year-old case of Chronic Fatigue Syndrome (CFS) began to improve. I believe anybody's health will improve if you drink this juice or something similar, daily. If you don't want to grow or buy sprouts, then any leafy green vegetables are a reasonable substitute. I also sometimes add garlic or turmeric or ginger or lemon to this juice to mix up the flavor and get an even bigger immune boost.

Ingredients:

- 1 large cucumber (organic, with skin)
- 5 or 6 large celery stalks (organic)
- ½ pound of fresh sunflower sprouts (green shoots)
- ½ to ¾ pound of fresh pea sprouts (green pea shoots)
- Garlic, lemon, ginger or turmeric (optional, to taste)

Directions:

Scrub and wash the cucumber and celery. Soak and rinse the pea and sunflower sprouts. Cut cucumber to fit in juicer and run everything through your juicer. Stir, sip and chew slowly.

In the Cabinet Under:

Immune booster, detoxification, general vitality. HHI Juice.

The Magic Shot – Wheatgrass Juice

Wheatgrass juice is the magic bullet at the Hippocrates Health Institute (HHI). The benefit in wheatgrass comes from its chlorophyll content. When you make a shot of wheatgrass, you'll see the profound dark green color of the chlorophyll. The nutrients in wheatgrass are so healthy because they are so easy for the body to assimilate (bio-available).

Some reasons why wheatgrass is good for you: one ounce of wheatgrass equals about two pounds of vegetables, wheatgrass contains more than 90 minerals needed by the body and more than 30 enzymes, due to the high chlorophyll content, wheatgrass oxygenates your blood; diseases, including cancer, cannot survive in oxygen-rich blood.

If you want to broaden the results of wheatgrass, you can use it as a rectal implant. At HHI we were taught to implant up to four ounces of wheatgrass juice twice daily during health challenges or periods of detox.

Ingredients:

2 handfuls of fresh wheatgrass – to make two ounces of juice

Directions:

Soak and rinse wheatgrass and run through your juicer. Sip and chew your wheatgrass juice. For maximum benefit, you must drink it immediately after juicing.

In the Cabinet Under:

Immune booster, detoxification, general vitality. HHI Juice.

Juice Remedies for Weight Loss, Detox, Energy, & Focus

Menu of Juices by Category

Use this quick reference section if you are looking for a juice to provide a nutrient boost to a particular area of your health.

Inflammation Reduction – Anti-Aging

Coconut Turmeric Recovery

Skin Care you Drink

Heavy Duty Detox

Prevent Defense

Live Long and Prosper

Cilantro Cholesterol Reduction

Cilantro Detox

Master Antioxidant

Workout, Hydration & Growing Muscle

Protein Building Juice

Coconut Turmeric Recovery

Rehydration Juice

Alkaline Hydration

Workout Booster Juice

Digestion System Aids

Gut Calming Juice

Sweet Potato Pineapple

Juicy Omega 3

Minty Digestive Ease

Tropical Enzyme Explosion

Healthy Ginger Ale

Blood Sugar Balance

Blood Sugar Balancer Take 2

Ulcer Relief

Inflammation Reducer

Martha Stewart's Green Juice

Hangover

Cucumber Hangover Handler

Bitter Melon Hangover Handler

Immune System Boosters

3 Karat Immunity

Prevent Defense

Healthy Spicy Tomato Juice

Brainy Green Immune Boost

Sweet Potato Pineapple

Blackcurrant Blood Pressure Relief

V9 Juice

Green Juice Phase One

Vitamin C Booster Juice

Immunity Mechanic

Master Antioxidant

Inflammation Reducer

Green Juice for Immunity

Salad on the Run

Healthy Skin

Skin Care you Drink

Facelift in a Glass

Live Long and Prosper

Acne Fighter

Overall Health Improvement

Salty Red Carrot

Ms. Healthy

Multivitamin in a Glass

V9 Juice

Green Juice Phase One

Red Dandelion for the Liver

Rehydration Juice

Liver Cleanse in a Glass

Dr. Oz's Green Juice

Juicing Recipe Cabinet

Salad on the Run

Jennifer Aniston's Green Juice

This Juice Changed my Life

The Magic Shot

Energy Drinks

All in the Family Energy Detox

Sweet Potato Pineapple

Coffee 2.0

Blood Sugar Balance

Blood Sugar Balancer Take 2

Breakfast with Benefits

Protein Building Juice

Hot & Spicy Energy

Nut Milk

Detox Juices

All in the Family Energy Detox

Heavy Duty Detox

Greens & Grapefruit

Ms. Healthy

Tasty Veggie Detox

Kale & Broccoli Detox

Hot & Spicy Energy

Parasite & Candida Detox Juice
Brain Detox Juice
Cilantro Cholesterol Reduction
Cilantro Detox
This Juice Changed my Life
The Magic Shot

Cancer Fighters

Healthy Spicy Tomato Juice
Ms. Healthy
Juicy Omega 3
Kale & Broccoli Detox
Tropical Enzyme Explosion
Women's Health Tonic
Cilantro Detox
Chlorophyll and Carotene
Citrus C Fighter
The Magic Shot

Lower Cholesterol & Hearth Health

Prevent Defense
Cholesterol Control
Cholesterol Corrector
Cilantro Cholesterol Reduction
Healthy Heart

Better than Milk

Weight Loss
Greens & Grapefruit

Healthy Heart

Workout Booster Juice

Mood, Memory, Alertness & Intelligence
Brainy Green Immune Boost

Breakfast with Benefits

Brain Detox Juice

Ginseng Concentration Improver

IQ Booster

The Big Brain Juice

Green Juice Depression Relief

Blood Pressure
Blackcurrant Blood Pressure Relief

Common Cold Zapper

Tropical Enzyme Explosion

Insomnia & Sleep
Insomnia Relief

Headaches, Colds, Flu & Fever
Common Cold Zapper

Shake the Cold - Warming Juice
Headache Relief
Migraine Relief Taco Juice
Cool that Fever Red
Cool that Fever Yellow
Fruity Flu Remedy
Flu Destroyer
Green Juice for Immunity
Dr. Oz's Green Juice

Bone Health & Osteoporosis
Multivitamin in a Glass
Better than Milk

Bladder, Kidney & Liver
Bladder Infection Fighter
Dandelion Diuretic
Red Dandelion for the Liver
Master Antioxidant
Liver Cleanse in a Glass

Woman's Health
Women's Health Tonic
Iron Woman

Folic Acid for Pregnancy

Iron – Anemia Aid

Sex Organs / Aphrodisiac

The George Clooney

Celebrity Juices

Dr. Oz's Green Juice

Martha Stewart's Green Juice

Jennifer Aniston's Green Juice

Juice Remedies for Weight Loss, Detox, Energy, & Focus

References

http://www.naturalnews.com/
http://www.healthyfoodhouse.com
http://www.whfoods.com/
http://www.dailymail.co.uk/
http://www.sigmaaldrich.com/
http://umm.edu/
http://www.theholykale.com/
http://www.alternet.org/
http://juicerecipes.com/
http://www.leaflady.org/
http://sacredsourcenutrition.com/
http://www.drweil.com/
http://www.thedailygreen.com/
http://www.cavemandoctor.com
http://myjuicecleanse.com/
http://www.dynamicgreens.com/

Manufactured by Amazon.ca
Bolton, ON